MIDLANDS
HALF-CAB BUSES
THE TWILIGHT
YEARS

MIKE RHODES

AMBERLEY

First published 2023

Amberley Publishing
The Hill, Stroud
Gloucestershire, GL5 4EP

www.amberley-books.com

Copyright © Mike Rhodes, 2023

The right of Mike Rhodes to be identified as
the Author of this work has been asserted in
accordance with the Copyrights, Designs and
Patents Act 1988.

ISBN 978 1 3981 1610 8 (print)
ISBN 978 1 3981 1611 5 (ebook)

British Library Cataloguing in Publication Data.
A catalogue record for this book is available from
the British Library.

Origination by Amberley Publishing.
Printed in the UK.

Introduction

When describing a bus as a half-cab it usually refers to the cab and engine compartment arrangement whereby the bodywork to the latter is cut away. This arrangement ensures warm air from the engine can escape into the atmosphere and the aerodynamics of the air passing over the engine shroud can help to keep the temperature down. Half-cab buses could be either single- or double-deckers and remained in production by a number of bodybuilders until the late 1960s, by which time the rear- or underfloor-engine bus had taken a firm foothold with most UK bus operators, largely brought about by the Government's bus grant scheme.

The Midlands is a vast area of the country and for the purpose of this volume I have included the following bus operators: the West Midlands PTE, the municipal operations of Derby, East Staffordshire District Council (Burton-upon-Trent), Leicester, Northampton and Nottingham and a representation of the extensive Midland Red fleet. Half-cabs were also operated by a number of independent bus companies dotted around the region. These included Stratford Blue, the Green Bus Company of Rugeley, Stevensons of Uttoxeter, W. Gash & Sons of Newark and South Notts of Gotham.

Reviewing the different operators in the above order, the West Midland PTE was formed on 1 October 1969 and initially absorbed the municipal bus fleets of Birmingham, Walsall, West Bromwich and Wolverhampton. These were later joined by buses from the NBC Midland Red operator's garages, which were based within the PTE area, in December 1973, and by Coventry's municipal buses in April 1974. The Birmingham contingent included some 650 'Standards' which had been new in 1950–54. These were buses that were bodied by different builders, primarily Metro-Cammell and Crossley Motors, but to a similar design as specified by the Transport Department. Five single-deck half-cabs, in the form of Weymann-bodied Leyland PS2s, also transferred to the PTE. Whilst the latter were quickly eliminated from the fleet the Standards continued in service, in diminishing numbers, until October 1977, with sixty-four of the type still available for service at the beginning of the Queen's Silver Jubilee year.

The Birmingham Standards in the main continued to operate on the city routes. However a number were transferred to Walsall to accelerate the abandonment of the town's trolleybus system, which was accomplished at the beginning of October 1970. Besides a selection of ancient Guys and Daimlers, Walsall had purchased a mixture of Daimler CVGs, Dennis Lolines and Regent Vs in 1960/1. Their final half-cab contribution was a batch of fifteen Metro-Cammell-bodied Daimler CVG6s, which were new in 1962. All of these sixties-bought buses were front entrance and the last of the configuration were again withdrawn in 1977.

West Bromwich, meanwhile, had settled on buying Daimler CVGs, which were invariably bodied by Metro-Cammell Weymann. In the region of ninety examples passed to the PTE, the newest of which dated from 1965. These were all rear-entrance buses. A number were later transferred to a handful of Birmingham garages and operated on city routes including the outer circular routes 11A and 11C. Meanwhile the buses acquired from Wolverhampton Corporation included some antiquated Brush and Park Royal-bodied Guy Arab IIIs, along with a mixture of full-fronted and half-cab Guy Arab IVs and Vs. The latter numbered some 164 examples, which had joined the fleet in 1957/63–67, mainly as trolleybus replacement vehicles, and had been variously bodied by Metro-Cammell, Park Royal, Strachans and Weymann. The last of the former West Bromwich and Wolverhampton half-cabs were withdrawn in 1978.

With the eight Midland Red garages transferred to the PTE in December 1973 came an assortment of ninety of the in-house-built D9s. Originally numbering 345 in the Midland Red fleet, they were of the conventional layout of having a traditional half-cab front and a doored-rear entrance. The three production series had been built at the Carlyle Works between 1960 and 1966. A few of these are also illustrated still working with the NBC's Midland Red company. Finally in April 1974 the PTE gained another large intake of half-cabs in the form of Coventry's extensive allocation of Metro-Cammell-bodied Daimler CVG6s, which numbered in the region of 110 buses. Like the West Bromwich Daimlers these too were to be seen on Birmingham's city routes. A handful of these lasted until 1979, which proved to be the year in which the half-cab bus was completely eliminated from the West Midlands PTE, having in the main been replaced by large numbers of Leyland Fleetlines.

The Coventry Daimler Works had a strong influence with regards to the type of bus purchased by the municipal fleets in the Midlands as Derby, East Staffs and Northampton all based their double-deck requirements in the 1960s on the ever-popular CVG6/CCG5 models. Derby Corporation had been another enthusiastic operator of trolleybuses. Like the Wolverhampton system, the Derby trolleybus system also closed in 1967. The first batch of Daimler CVG6s was purchased in 1957 and these were bodied by Park Royal. Further batches followed in each of the years 1961–64/66, all of which were bodied by Charles Roe. The last order was somewhat unusual in that it was a mixture of CVGs and rear-engined Fleetlines. In 1973 Derby acquired Blue Bus Services of nearby Willington and another five half-cabs joined the fleet. The last of the original half-cabs were withdrawn in 1980.

East Staffordshire District Council, which was the former Burton-upon-Trent Corporation, was a fairly modest-sized bus operator. Thirty-five buses were transferred to the newly named fleet of which fourteen were half-cabs in the form of Massey-bodied Daimler CCG5s. Two more half-cabs were added to the fleet in 1975 with the purchase of two former Wigan Corporation Leyland PD2A/27s. Three of the Daimlers continued in service until 1981. Equally long-lived were Leicester City Transport's half-cab buses of which there was a considerable number, mainly of Leyland manufacture although there was also a smattering of AEC types in the shape of Bridgemasters and Renowns. The body types specified included East Lancashire Coachbuilders, Metro-Cammell and Park Royal. The last of these bowed out with due ceremony on 2 October 1982.

For uniformity Northampton was the place to visit. Over an eleven-year period, between 1957 and 1968, the council specified the exact same model of bus, the rear-entrance Roe-bodied Daimler CVG6, which was bought in small numbers year upon year, eventually amounting to sixty-eight of the type. These buses dominated the town's bus services throughout the 1960s and well into the 1970s. The last regular operational buses of the type were not withdrawn until 1982.

The last municipal operator featured in this book is Nottingham City Transport. Latterly NCT operated half-cab buses, which were a mixture of Park Royal-bodied AEC Regent Vs, MCCW-bodied Leyland PD2/40s and AEC Renowns with similar-looking bodies but built by three different bodybuilders. The latter followed several batches of PDR1/2 Atlanteans and were purchased in 1965. These had relatively short lives with the undertaking as all three types were eliminated from the fleet in 1976. Nottingham had purchased four half-cab single-deck buses in 1951 in the form of East Lancs-bodied AEC Regal IIIs; these lasted in service until 1969. Nottingham City Transport was still municipally owned at the time of writing.

As previously mentioned there were a number of well-known independent operators throughout the region. Stratford Blue was a longstanding name in the industry but was absorbed by Midland Red in January 1971. Six former Stratford Blue Willowbrook-bodied Leyland PD3A/1s had a brief stay of execution with Midland Red before they were withdrawn in 1972 and then sold on to Isle of Man Road Services, with whom they clocked up another ten years of service. Harper Bothers of Heath Hayes was another well-known operator, which passed to Midland Red in September 1974 and latterly operated a small number of half-cab Leyland Titans. South Notts of Gotham was another notable independent operator with an eclectic mix of mainly second-hand buses, which included a number of half-cabs. Whilst the last of these were eliminated in the 1970s the company was later bought out, in March 1991, by Nottingham City Transport.

Of some significance in the independent group was Stevensons of Uttoxeter. Stevensons was first established in 1926 with a depot in the small village of Spath. By the early 1970s around forty buses were owned, including several second-hand half-cabs. They remained a moderately sized operator until merging with nearby East Staffordshire District Council on 1 October 1985. The name was phased out in 1997 by which time the enlarged operator had become part of the Arriva Group.

This book is a collection of the author's own pictures which record the Midland's bus scene in the 1970s. Half-cab buses in the UK have been a thing of the past for several decades now, although there are numerous preserved examples which can be viewed, and ridden upon, at the many vintage transport centres that are dotted around the UK. A poignant thought for the reader is that quite a number of pictures contained within the book were recorded during the Queen's Silver Jubilee year and these are only now seeing the light of day more than forty-five years later, the year after the Queen celebrated her Platinum Jubilee – how time passes.

Mike Rhodes

Two of Birmingham City Transport's iconic 'Standards', Nos 3054 and 3030, are seen in Lordswood Road at Harborne on 24 August 1976. By this time, generally confined to peak time extras and the outer circular routes, the two 1953-built Metro-Cammell-bodied Guy Arab IVs are seen working the 11A and 11C respectively.

Standard No. 3206 was one of the last to be built in 1954 and was a Daimler CVG6 completed with a Crossley-built fifty-five-seat rear-entrance body. It was photographed in City Road in Smethwick on 4 April 1977 – the last year of operation of the Birmingham Standards.

Above and below: Friday 28 February 1975 in central Birmingham and there are still half-cab buses to be seen on a regular basis. A number of city routes showed different route numbers depending on the direction of travel. Daimler CVG6 No. 3191 (above) has stopped in busy Corporation Street on its journey from Hall Green to the Pheasey estate; it ran as the 91 in the opposite direction. Meanwhile similar vehicle No. 3176 (below) was recorded alongside Snow Hill railway station on the 92, which was also part of the 90/1 group but operated via Stratford Road as opposed to Baldwins Lane. The PTE adopted the same livery layout for the Standards, albeit with a lighter blue, to that used by the previous city transport department. Even the khaki roof was retained. Whilst No. 3176 was withdrawn later that year, No. 3191 lasted until 1977.

Also seen on 28 February 1975 is Crossley-bodied Daimler CVG6 No. 2846 in Soho Hill at Hockley. The buildings in the background were all still standing in 2021 including the former Palladium Cinema (far left), although it presented a somewhat derelict picture.

The last regular cross-city route to be operated by the Standards was the 15/16, which ran from Hamstead in the north to Whittington Oval at Lea Hall. Daimler CVG6s Nos 2788/78 are seen at the Oval terminus on Monday 16 February 1976. This is no longer a terminal point.

A little later in the year, on 19 May 1976, Daimler CVG6 No. 2862 was also photographed at the Oval terminus. Note the Birmingham Corporation Bundy (Timing) Clock opposite the rear platform. The clocks were made by the Bundy Manufacturing Company of Binghampton (New York), USA. The route was converted to 'OPO' later in the year.

Daimler CVG6 No. 2778 is seen again on 16 February 1976 at the Hamstead end of route 15. The stylish Bundy Clock can again be seen in this picture. By 2022 this was no longer a bus terminus but route 16, which ran from Great Barr to the city centre, still served the stop.

Metro-Cammell-bodied Guy Arab IV No. 3022 was caught on camera in City Road at Smethwick on 4 April 1977 as it made its way round the 27-mile-long clockwise outer circular route. Taking nearly two and a half hours to complete the circle, in the region of fifteen buses would have been required for each direction of travel. A similar number of buses were still employed in 2022.

Only ten days before the last of Birmingham's Standards were withdrawn Guy Arab IV No. 3015 was caught on a peak-time extra on route 32 in New Street in the city centre. This would have been an Acocks Green garage duty. Following behind is former Midland Red Alexander-bodied Daimler Fleetline No. 6264. Wimpy bars were all the rage in the 1970s.

On 19 May 1976 Guy Arab IV No. 3013 was photographed resting in Crossfield Road opposite Lea Hall garage whilst about to undertake training duties. The garage had been opened in April 1955. It was closed by National Express West Midlands in July 2010 but the building was still standing in 2021.

On the same day Daimler CVG6 No. 2870 was photographed in Ethel Street, in the city centre, whilst negotiating one of Birmingham's one-way systems. The Pancake House has now become Byrons Hamburgers and the street has since been pedestrianised.

Above and below: Two pictures illustrating the workings of the outer circular routes 11A and 11C as recorded on Monday 4 April 1977. *Above:* Crossley-bodied Daimler CVG6 No. 2858 skirts along Lordswood Road in the affluent district of Harborne. It is passing house number 300, which has been vastly altered since this picture was taken. *Below*: Just a short distance away Daimler CVG6 No. 3155 and former West Bromwich Corporation Daimler No. 255H are both waiting time in the shadow of The King's Head public house, which is situated on the corner of Hagley Road. Number 255H was one of a batch of six Metro-Cammell-bodied CVG6s which were new to West Bromwich Corporation in 1964. It was withdrawn later that year along with the last Birmingham Standards. This location was also used for crew changes.

Metro-Cammell-bodied Guy Arab IV No. 3031 catches the sun as it turns from Watford Road into Pershore Road at Cotteridge on 24 August 1976. This was the furthest south the route penetrated before heading off east. The bus is displaying very untidy blind arrangements. The corner shop is now a Subway eatery.

Crew are in discussion with an inspector as Guy Arabs Nos 3030 and 2934 prepare to swap over on the 11C. This picture was recorded in Lordswood Road at Harborne on 24 August 1976. Across the road is Lonsdale Road, which led to the main entrance of Harborne garage. The garage was closed in 1986 and the site is now occupied by residential flats.

Crossley-bodied Daimler CVG6 No. 2826 makes a fine sight as it travels down Sandon Road at Bearwood on 4 April 1977. It is passing house number 69 (blue gates), which along with many of the houses along this road have somewhat changed in appearance (for the better) over the intervening forty-five years.

Daimler CVG6 No. 3225 is seen in New Road at Handsworth on 18 October 1977. The electrified line above swings round to Perry Barr and Witton and was often used by trains on diversion around the Birmingham environs. The line in the distance was a second side of a triangle and led round to Hamstead station on the line to Walsall. The advertising hoarding has subsequently been removed.

Guy Arab IV No. 3068 has clearly seen better days as it displays patches of flaking paint. It is seen in Boulton Road at Handsworth on 18 October 1977. The lady on the open platform will be alighting at the stop round the corner in Soho Road. A former West Bromwich Daimler CVG6 is seen heading towards the photographer on the 11A. The open land on the right is now a surfaced car park.

Another classic rear-end view depicts Daimler CVG6 No. 3223 waiting at the Yew Tree bus stop in Church Road at Yardley on 24 August 1976. Unfortunately the trees have now gone and the Yew Tree pub, which has undergone a complete rebuild and is just visible on the corner of Hob Moor Road, is now known as The Clumsy Swan.

The elderly gentleman pedestrian has to do a double take (although his wife takes no notice) as he tries to comprehend the age of 1951 Guy Arab IV No. 2600, which was still plying its trade through the city centre twenty-five years later. This scene was captured in Colmore Row on 24 August 1976. The closest route to the Oval from the city is now National Express West Midlands service 97, which runs from Albert Street to Chelmsley Wood. This is still a bus stand for city services.

On the same day Daimler CVG6 No. 3121 was photographed in the wide expanse of leafy Harborne Park Road at Harborne. The popularity of the outer circular routes is adequately demonstrated by the well-loaded bus, which resulted in a fairly frequent schedule.

West Bromwich Corporation had favoured the Daimler CVG6 since 1952 and a significant number passed to the PTE. Number 225H was a 30-foot-long version with a Metro-Cammell body. The longer CVG6-30 model was prevalent in the fleet of Kowloon Motor Bus. Number 225H was photographed in West Bromwich bus station on 28 February 1975.

Seen on the same day is Willowbrook-bodied No. 194H, which dated from 1957. The letter 'H' was simply added to the corporation fleet number by the PTE with 'L' 'N', and 'Y' being added to the buses of the other former corporation fleets. The bus is waiting to depart for nearby Wednesbury via the direct route through Black Lake.

A number of the West Bromwich Daimlers were transferred to Birmingham city garages for use on peak-time extras and the outer circulars. Number 248H is seen in Stephenson Street in the city centre on 19 May 1976 working through to Whittington Oval. Note the upper destination screen has been blanked off.

Number 241H was a year older than the bus depicted above having joined the West Bromwich fleet in 1962. It is seen in Boulton Road at Handsworth on 18 October 1977. Although the last of the Birmingham Standards were withdrawn ten days later, the outer circular routes were not converted to 'OPO' until the following March.

Number 216H was one of a batch of six Daimler buses purchased by West Bromwich in 1958. It is seen in Winson Green Road, near Winson Green Prison, on 18 October 1977 on what would appear to be a short working of the 11C. The area would appear to have changed significantly since this picture was taken.

Number 253H of 1964 is seen in Station Road at Stetchford on 24 June 1977 on the 11A. This particular branch of Barclays bank was one of many to have been closed over recent years. Ironically the building, on the corner of Lyndon Road, was a *Cash Generator* establishment in 2021.

West Bromwich Daimler No. 248H is seen again, this time in City Road in Smethwick on 4 April 1977. These buses seemed to be unable to display the suffix letter but the author's notes record the bus as working the anti-clockwise circuit and is approaching the junction of Portland Road. This bus is now preserved as West Bromwich No. 248.

Similar bus No. 247H, working from Hockley garage, was photographed in New Street in the city centre on 24 August 1976 on a peak-time extra on service 16. In the distance is former Midland Red D9 No. 5438, which is working from Stourbridge garage. Both buses were withdrawn the following year.

Number 240(H) was caught in Stephenson Street in the city centre on 19 May 1976 with a working to Whittington Oval. Repainting of the original corporation constituent bus fleets also included the provision of a khaki roof, deemed to be a better weather protectorate, which Birmingham Corporation had introduced after the Second World War.

The last Daimler CVG6s purchased by West Bromwich Corporation were again 30 footers and comprised Nos 259–65, in 1965. Number 260H is seen departing West Bromwich bus station for the Yew Tree Estate on 30 March 1976. These longer buses were a H74R configuration with an additional four seats on each deck.

Numerically last of all, No. 265H was similarly photographed in West Bromwich bus station on 30 March 1976 on another local town route to Princes End via Wood Lane. West Bromwich bus station is still in the same location, although it has been reconfigured.

The D9 was Midland Red's last in-house mass-produced double-decker and amounted to 345 examples over a six-year period between 1960 and 1966. Ninety of the type were transferred to the PTE in December 1973. Number 5023 is seen in Oldbury bus station on 19 May 1976 on route 229, which ran from Bearwood to Blackheath. This D9 was withdrawn the following year whilst bus routes in Oldbury now use on-street bus stands in Halesowen Street.

Number 5326 was new in 1963 and was photographed in Hill Street in Birmingham city centre on 19 May 1976. Route 130 ran from Stourbridge to Birmingham via Halesowen. John Bright Street on the right has since been pedestrianised whilst the building behind the bus has been renovated and incorporated in a larger modern structure. The D9 was withdrawn later in the year and sold for scrap.

Number 4981 was allocated to Stourbridge garage when it was photographed in Dudley bus station on 4 April 1977. Route 245 ran from Wednesbury to Stourbridge via Tipton, Dudley and Brierley Hill. A reconfigured bus station remained on the same site in 2022. Number 4981 was withdrawn five months later and sold for scrap. The service number 245 could still be seen at Dudley on Rotala Diamond buses running to Sedgley.

Above and below: Dudley bus station was and still is a busy location for bus movements. On 19 May 1976 a collection of Daimler Fleetlines and former Midland Red D9s could be found. *Above*: Number 5439 is showing route 246 on the blind, which will take it to Stourbridge, and alongside is new MCW Leyland Fleetline No. 6314. Standing on the hill is Dudley Castle, which dates from the thirteenth to fourteenth centuries having been rebuilt after the original castle was demolished on the orders of King Henry II. *Below*: Parked up amongst the ranks is D9 No. 4900, which was new in 1961. Both the D9s were withdrawn the following year and sold to breakers yards. The D9 was a truly in-house-built machine and was powered by BMMO's own six-cylinder 10.5-litre KL engine, which was more powerful than the engine used in its predecessor, the D7.

Twenty-seven former Coventry Daimlers were transferred to Birmingham area garages in 1974/5 and renumbered into the 12xx series. Number 1263, which was new to Coventry Corporation in 1958, was photographed in Wellington Road in the district of Handsworth on 30 March 1976. It is approaching the junction of Hamstead Road on the anti-clockwise outer circular route.

Similar bus No. 307Y of 1961 is seen opposite the shops in Roseberry Avenue in the Coventry district of Bell Green on 24 June 1977. Route 8A worked from Bell Green across the city centre to Tile Hill. Note the letter 'S' below the destination screen, which is the garage code and denoted Sandy Lane. All odd numbered buses were allocated to Sandy Lane and even numbered buses to Harnall Lane.

MCCW-bodied Daimler CVG6 No. 336Y is seen in Hockley Lane at Eastern Green on 24 June 1977. Although the bus stop still exists, the pole and flag have been changed. This section of road is now served by National Express West Midlands route 14, which runs beyond Eastern Green to the University of Warwick.

Seen in the final simplified version of the Coventry Corporation livery are Daimlers Nos 266Y and 258Y, both of which are allocated to Harnall Lane garage. They were photographed in Hales Street, once a busy section of tramway, nearing the city centre on 24 June 1977. The majority of these buses were withdrawn in 1977/8, leaving just ten in service at the beginning of 1979.

A classic rear-end view of a Metro-Cammell-bodied back-loader of the 1960s. Former Coventry Corporation Daimler No. 276Y is seen in Hilmorton Road at Wood End. This scene has changed somewhat in that the building to the left has been replaced with new houses, the flats have been renovated with a new roof and the bus stop has been relocated. Route 21 Willenhall to Wood End still served the area in 2022.

Number 305Y is seen in Bushberry Avenue at the junction of Jardine Crescent in the Coventry district of Tile Hill (it would next work through to Bell Green on the opposite side of the city). The locality looks much the same today other than the large tree has been felled.

Daimlers Nos 327Y and 317Y are seen leaving Pool Meadow bus station on 19 May 1976. The two buses are heading out to separate 'Greens' and at 12.40 p.m. if the clock is to be believed. Pool Meadow still functions as a bus station, although only a small amount of the original still exists and that doesn't include the quaint-looking buildings on the left.

This view of Pool Meadow is much the same today other than the type of bus to be found. Daimler No. 283Y was waiting to depart for Tile Hill on 24 June 1977. The split destination display style was used by a number of bus operators for maximum effect. This particular bus did not see the year out.

A busy scene in Trinity Street in Coventry city centre on 24 June 1977 sees Daimler Nos 304Y and 328Y on local city routes. Buses still call at on-street stands in this thoroughfare and the adjacent building is now a Sainsbury's store. Trinity Street was previously known as New Buildings.

The driver of No. 308Y is in the middle of a conversation with his conductor, who has been distracted by passengers clambering aboard his bus. This is Trinity Street again on 19 May 1976. The upper part of Trinity Street has since been pedestrianised.

Number 290Y is seen at the Wyken terminus outside the Coventry Oak public house (now known as the New Pippin), which is situated at the junction of Hipswell Highway and Ansty Road. It would have worked across the city centre to Earlsdon.

1963-built example No. 335Y was photographed at the Tile Hill Village terminus located in Torrington Avenue at the junction of Station Avenue. Coventry Corporation's route numbering system was very straightforward, using the numbers 1 to 34. Three years on from the absorption by the PTE and the system remained largely unchanged, with the Daimler back-loaders regularly employed on routes 7, 8/8A, 9/9A, 10, 12, 19, 21 and 22.

Above and below: As previously mentioned a number of Coventry's Daimlers were reallocated to Birmingham area garages including these two, which were gainfully employed on the outer circular routes on 4 April 1977. *Above:* Working its way round anti-clockwise was No. 1233, which was captured in City Road at Smethwick as it passed the junction of Sandon Road. The highway trees have since been felled. *Below:* Travelling the opposite way round the circuit was No. 1220, which is seen in Lordswood Road at Harborne. Both buses were new in 1958, with No. 1220 being taken out of service later that year and No. 1233 the following year. Note the absence of any adverts, which were generally uncommon on Birmingham buses.

Walsall Corporation's last half-cab buses were a batch of fifteen MCCW-bodied Daimler CVG6s, which were purchased in 1963, the last of which were withdrawn in 1977. No. 75L is seen in St Paul's Street opposite Walsall bus station on 30 March 1976. The adjacent building was the rear of Woolworths with the frontage on Park Street. A modernised Walsall bus station still occupies this site.

Another of the batch, No. 65L, is seen in Bloxwich Road on the same day and is parked across from the Birchills' former Corporation bus garage. Note the quirky local destination of 'New Invention'. This Daimler was withdrawn later in the year. Part of the garage was still in use by National Express West Midlands in 2022.

Above and below: Walsall Corporation had a large combined fleet of buses and trolleybuses approaching nearly 250 in number with a sizeable garage at Birchills to house them all. The garage was built adjacent to an electric tram depot, which was in use from 1904 to 1933. *Above:* No. 78N was a Weymann-bodied Guy Arab V which had originated with Wolverhampton Corporation and was one of a large batch of forty obtained in 1963 as trolleybus replacement vehicles. *Below:* Indigenous to the depot was former Walsall Corporation Daimler No. 61L. Both buses were recorded on 31 March 1976.

Above and below: A visitor to Wolverhampton in the 1970s, on leaving the station, would immediately have been confronted by Railway Street (now Drive) bus station, which played host to many of the Black Country inter-town services. *Above:* On 28 February 1975 former Wolverhampton Corporation 1965-built Metro-Cammell-bodied Guy Arab V No. 158N was waiting to leave for Wombourn(e), 4 and a half miles to the south-west. *Below:* Similar vintage Guy Arab No. 170N is seen with former Midland Red Alexander-bodied Daimler Fleetline No. 6126 on 30 March 1976. Although the bus station closed many years ago, the land has only recently been built on with an adjacent extension to the Midland Metro opening in 2022. Towering above in the background is the Prince Albert Hotel, which was opened by Eley's Stafford Brewery Ltd in 1900 and is still functioning.

Two Weymann-bodied Guy Arab Vs, Nos 107N and 110N, from the same 1963 batch are seen in Queen Street in the centre of Wolverhampton on 30 March 1976. The adjacent building is the Old County Court, which dates from 1815. Queen Street is now a one-way street in the opposite direction.

Seen on 4 April 1977 is No. 164N, a 1965 Metro-Cammell-bodied Guy Arab V, which was recorded in Lichfield Street. Tettenhall Wood is situated in the west of the city and is still served by National Express route 10. Little has changed in this view and even the barber shop's sign is still insitu but minus its red markings. Preedy's Tobacconists is now Manders Estates.

Above and below: *Above:* Similar vehicle No. 161N, another former Wolverhampton Corporation Guy Arab V, was found in the company of Leyland National No. 4520, which was new to the PTE in 1974 in Dudley bus station on 4 April 1977. Virtually all of Wolverhampton's double-deck stock were of Guy manufacture since the bodybuilder was based in the city; the factory closed in 1982. Meanwhile No. 161N was withdrawn later in the year with the last of the type surviving into 1978. *Below:* Walsall's Daimlers could also be seen in Dudley working in on route 265 via Wednesbury. Number 75L is seen in the shadow of Dudley Castle on 19 May 1976. The former Corporation fleet's buses didn't suit the PTE livery and seemed to present a rundown appearance. As can be seen this batch of buses received the khaki roof embellishment.

Above and below: Acocks Green was a change-over point for crews on the outer circular routes as portrayed in these two views. *Above:* With the garage visible in the background 1953 Metro-Cammell-bodied Guy Arab IV No. 2962 is ready to depart Westley Road on 16 February 1976, a bleak winter's day, with a fresh crew on board. *Below:* Later in the year, in warmer climes, the drivers of 1954 Metro-Cammell-bodied Guy Arab IV No. 3068 are in the process of changing over. An inspector is also in attendance as Guy No. 2905 departs the garage to take up service on the 11C.

Also seen on 16 February 1976, across the road from Acocks Green garage, is 1953 Crossley-bodied Daimler CVG6 No. 3129, which is waiting in Fox Hollies Road. The two ladies are somewhat hesitant as to whether to board the bus or not. The petrol filling station is now a used car lot.

On the same day 1951 Metro-Cammell-bodied Guy Arab IV No. 2606 was photographed on its descent of the Bull Ring to Digbeth in Birmingham city centre. This area is now submerged under the revamped Bull Ring. Visible on the left is the Rotunda, which was opened in 1965 and is still a prominent feature on the Birmingham skyline.

Above and below: Acocks Green garage, along with Harborne, Selly Oak and Perry Barr, was one of Birmingham Corporation's new generation of bus garages and was opened in June 1928. It was still in use by National Express West Midlands in 2022. It has also provided buses for the outer circular routes over many years. Typifying its allocation of bus types for more than two decades are these two Birmingham Standards'. *Above:* Daimler CVG6 No. 3166 is seen on 16 February 1976. *Below:* Guy Arab No. 2905 was receiving last-minute checks on 24 August 1976.

Seen on 16 February 1976 in Colmore Row making its way to the Whittington Oval at Yardley is 1951-built Metro-Cammell-bodied Guy Arab IV No. 2580. Colmore Row leads into Victoria Square, both of which have been pedestrianised at the locations shown in the above and below views. The passengers are given very specific instructions as to how to queue for their bus.

One of the oldest Standards still in service in 1976 was Guy Arab No. 2533 of 1950, which was latterly based at Acocks Green garage. It is seen on 24 August rounding Victoria Square in the city centre on its journey from Hamstead to Yardley. It remained in service right to the end of Standard operation and then passed into preservation. It is passing what is known as Birmingham Town Hall, a concert hall, which was opened in 1834.

Moving away from the city centre and 1952 example Crossley-bodied Daimler CVG6 No. 2792 is seen outside the Beaufort Arms in Old Walsall Road at Hamstead on 30 March 1976. The original pub was established in the 1860s but was replaced by the present incumbent prior to the Second World War. It was still functioning in 2022.

Photographed on the same day at the Hamstead terminus was 1951-built Metro-Cammell-bodied Guy Arab IV No. 2609. The 15/16 routes were worked by Perry Barr and Lea Hall garages. This is no longer a bus terminus but looked much the same in 2022, although most of the houses now have modern windows.

Above and below: On occasions large bus fleets would retain withdrawn buses and use them for other auxiliary uses. On 26 February 1976 two such vehicles were to be found in the garage yard at Perry Barr. *Above:* Carrying the number 95 Metro-Cammell-bodied Guy Arab V JOJ 991 had been No. 2991 in the WMPTE fleet. Delivered to Birmingham Corporation in March 1953, it had been withdrawn from PSV use as long ago as 1971. *Below:* Also in use as a service vehicle was MOF 13, originally No. 3013 and renumbered to 13. It was four months younger than No. 2991 and had only been withdrawn the previous year. Clearly evident in the broadside view is the straight staircase leading to the upper deck. It is not clear what function these two buses performed in this guise.

Above and below: On 4 April 1977 these two views were recorded of Standards alongside public houses in the Harborne district of Birmingham. *Above:* Guy Arab No. 2940, new in 1952, was photographed in Lordswood Road passing the Old House At Home situated on the corner of Gillhurst Road. *Below:* A short distance away at the junction of Hagley Road West was the King's Head where similar bus No. 2958 was found taking a breather from its arduous journey around the outer environs of Birmingham. After giving sterling service for many years the majority of the last Standards were broken up in the Yorkshire scrapyards of Barnsley and Rotherham. Both pubs were still part of the hospitality scene in 2022.

The Outer Circular routes were often supplemented by part-route workings, which would display 11E (Extra). One such working is portrayed by Daimler CVG6 No. 3191, which was photographed in Hagley Road at Harborne on 4 April 1977 on a clockwise extra which was only going as far as Erdington Six Ways.

Another clockwise working was seen in Stoney Lane at Yardley to the east of the city centre on 24 August 1976. A very well-loaded Daimler CVG6, No. 3137, is approaching the junction of Hob Moor Road/Church Road with passengers even standing on the back platform.

On a dull day in June 1977 Daimler CVG6 No. 3155 is seen in Brookvale Road at Witton. It is crossing the River Tame and has just pulled away from the Deykin Road bus stop. The bus stop has since been moved to the opposite side of the bridge and the tall brick building behind the bus has since been demolished. The brick gable ends are, however, still standing.

Similar bus No. 3166 was photographed on 30 March 1976, turning from Soho Road into Rookery Road. This cosmopolitan district of Birmingham has changed little over the years. However, Withers Newsagent & Tobacconists is now a Universal Foodstore whilst Enus is now Ashta Jewellers. A pedestrian guardrail has also been erected behind the kerbline.

Also seen on 30 March 1976 was Crossley-bodied Daimler No. 2831 in Handsworth Wood Road. It is approaching the Church Lane/Hamstead Road roundabout. Little has changed in this Birmingham locality.

Seen travelling in the opposite direction on route 15/16, Daimler No. 2792 was photographed in Hill Street in the city centre on 19 May 1976. It is outside what is now known as the Railway Bar. The Grapes had a relatively short existence as an alcohol repository and functioned as such from 1966 to 1987; it is now a convenience store.

Birmingham was the only major Midlands operator to still use any single-deck half-cabs into the 1970s. In 1950 the Corporation purchased thirty Weymann-bodied Leyland PS2/1s and five of these transferred to the PTE in 1969. Number 2260 survived in service until 1972. However No. 2257, which was withdrawn in May 1969, was retained as a Driver Tuition Vehicle and Breakdown Tow Bus. It was finally delicensed in December 1978 and passed into preservation. Seen at Perry Barr garage on 26 February 1977.

Derby Corporation was another Midlands municipal bus operator that favoured Daimler products. Number 159 was new in 1964 and was one of fifty Roe-bodied Daimler CVG6s which were purchased new from 1961 to 1966. Still in the old olive green and cream with no fleet markings, it was photographed in the Corn Market on 24 May 1975. Number 159 was withdrawn in 1979. The Corn Market has since been pedestrianised and the adjacent retailer is Primark.

Above and below: Derby Corporation opened a new garage in Ascot Drive in 1949; it also played host to trolleybuses until the system closed on 9 September 1967. The livery was changed radically from olive green to light blue and grey in May 1969. *Above:* Number 160 was new in 1964 and still sported the old colours when photographed on 24 May 1975. It continued in service until 1979. *Below:* The new livery still incorporated the borough coat of arms but the fleet name was straight to the point and the lettering must have been the largest seen on any fleet in the country. The final Daimler, No. 189, is seen in the garage yard on 24 September 1977.

Above and below: Derby's central bus station (off Station Approach) was designed by the Borough Architect, Charles Herbert Aslin (1893–1959), and opened in 1933. *Above:* Three Daimler CVG6s, Nos 134/69/85, can be seen in the same shot recorded on 24 August 1976, although the livery arrangement differs on one of them. Note also the chrome bumpers on the back. These buses were withdrawn between 1976 and 1978. The bus station closed in October 2005 and a new bus station opened on the same site in March 2010. *Below:* Laying over at the back of the bus station on the same day was 1964-built example No. 158. In both views all the windows are open, which reflects on the long hot summer of '76. What had officially been declared a drought ended the following month.

The classic rear view of a Charles Roe-bodied open-platform Daimler CVG6 seen on Derby No. 189 as it turns from Albert Street into St Peter's Street on 24 August 1976. This was the last of the type received by the undertaking in 1966 and remained in service until 1978. The Midland Bank is now HSBC and Marks & Spencer has become a Tesco Metro. St Peter's Street is now pedestrianised.

One of the 1961-built batch, No. 127, was photographed in the Corn Market on the same day on local route 33 to Upper Dale Road to the south of the city. More change to the retail shops as Ratners is now the British Heart Foundation and Dorothy Perkins has become Iman Hair & Beauty.

Number 169 was photographed in the Market Place again on 24 August 1976. This is another city centre street which has since been pedestrianised. The imposing entrance is unmistakably the Guildhall (Theatre).

On the same day No. 165 of the same batch is followed across Exeter Bridge, over the River Derwent, by a Plaxton-bodied Bedford SB, one of eight registered RNL992-9 which were originally new to Armstrong's of Westerhope near Newcastle in 1960. Both this Daimler and the one featured above were withdrawn in 1977.

A line-up of out-of-service buses parked up at the bus station. From left to right they are Willowbrook-bodied Daimler SRC No. 259, one of a batch of five new in 1972, Daimler CVG6s Nos 151/2 and Roe-bodied Daimler CRG No. 184. All four buses were withdrawn between 1978 and 1980.

Number 156 was the last bus in service to wear the olive green and cream livery and was withdrawn in these colours in 1978. It was also unusual in receiving the large DERBY fleet name, which was usually reserved for repaints. This view, taken at Ascot Drive, is dated 24 May 1975. Since 1996 the depot has been under the control of Arriva and was still in use in 2022 to house a fleet of around 150 buses.

Above and below: On 1 December 1973 Derby Corporation acquired the business of Blue Bus Services (Tailby & George) of nearby Willington and continued to operate the company as a subsidiary. The fleet comprised twenty-five vehicles including three low-height Willowbrook-bodied Daimler CVG6/CD650s. In the mid-1970s these were often gainfully employed on the service from Burton to Derby (a low bridge at Willington dictated the use of low-height buses). *Above*: Daimler CVG6 No. 34, new in 1960, is seen in Burton Wetmore Road bus station on 24 May 1975. *Below*: Similar vehicle No. 31 of 1955 at Derby on the same day. On the night of 5 January 1976 a disastrous fire at the Willington garage wiped the whole fleet out except for two buses which had been garaged at Derby overnight – Nos 31/2.

Burton-upon-Trent Corporation became East Staffordshire District Council Transport (ESDC) on 1 April 1974. Not only did the undertaking change its name but it also radically changed its fleet colours. A moderate-sized fleet of thirty-five vehicles, which included fourteen Massey-bodied Daimler CCG5 Daimler half-cabs. No. 88 is seen in Burton High Street on 24 September 1977; new in 1964, it lasted in service until 1981. Cantors is now Haynes Furnishers whilst the adjacent building with the scaffolding has since been demolished.

After initially painting the roofs of the buses green the operator switched to blue in 1976. Daimler No. 100 is seen in Station Road in the town centre on 29 May 1979. In the intervening forty-three years Woodhouse has become a Ryman stationery outlet and the road has been pedestrianised.

Daimler No. 91 was new in 1964 and gave thirteen years of service to ESDC. It is seen in Station Street on 24 May 1975. The adjacent shop is now Sunny Dee's Tanning Studio whilst the building behind the bus has since been demolished.

Number 97 of 1966 was photographed in Stapenhill Road on its way to Edge Hill on 24 September 1977. It is approaching the junction of St Peter's Street with the church of the same name in the background; the present building dates from 1881.

Above and below: At one time Burton was considered to be the brewing capital of the UK, with its own internal railway system around the town that connected the breweries with the distribution sidings on the main line. The network included numerous level crossings, which played havoc with the movement of local traffic. Did the local bus schedules include time for delays waiting at level crossings? Route 2 operated from the Edge Hill estate in the south of the town to Beam Hill in the north. Seen on 24 September 1977 are late 1960s Daimlers No. 101 (above) in Sycamore Road at Edge Hill and No. 93 (below) at the other end of the route outside the Beacon Hotel in Tutbury Road. The local bus operator in Burton in 2022 was Midland Classic, which was acquired by Rotala plc later that year.

Above and below: Two more pictures recorded on 24 September 1977. The garage was situated in Horninglow Street and was originally opened in June 1906 as a tram depot. *Above*: Daimler CCG5s Nos 89 and 94 stand ready for service. *Below*: In 1975 ESDC acquired two former Selnec (ex-Wigan Corporation) Northern Counties-bodied Leyland PD2A/27s. The former No. 3249 (Wigan No. 131), now ESDC No. 7, was also tucked away inside the garage. This bus had a short life with ESDC and was withdrawn in 1978.

Daimler No. 99 had been new in 1966. It was photographed in St Mary's Drive on 24 September 1977; Rolleston Road is in the background. This area is now served by the former Midland Classic (Diamond East Midlands) route 9, which runs from Queens Hospital to Midlands Gateway.

Number 93 again photographed in Burton High Street. Behind is former Portsmouth City Transport MCCW-bodied Leyland PDR1/1 No. 216, now ESDC No. 3, which was one of four acquired in 1976. Although pedestrianised, this section of the High Street remained largely unchanged in 2022 and even the NatWest bank was still open. The East Staff's Daimlers were replaced by East Lancs-bodied Dennis Dominators over a three-year period from 1978 to 1981. ESDC merged with Stevensons of Uttoxeter on 1 October 1985.

Above and below: Leicester City Transport operated out of a depot in Abbey Park Road, which first opened as a tram depot in May 1904. A new adjacent garage was built for buses in 1926; this was enlarged in 1934. In the 1960s/70s the undertaking operated a large stable of half-cab PD3 Titans. *Above:* On Saturday 21 September 1974 this group of buses comprised No. 400 (originally No. 162), a 1958 Park Royal-bodied Leyland PD3/1 in use as a Driver Tuition Vehicle; No. 167, a similar dated Titan but with a Metro-Cammell body (similar to Blackpool Corporation's PD3/1s except they were full-fronted); and No. 248, a 1961 Metro-Cammell-bodied Leyland PD3A/1. These three were successively withdrawn over the years 1974–76. *Below:* 1966-built Park Royal-bodied Leyland PD3A/1 No. 61 – withdrawn in 1980.

Above and below: Two pictures recorded on 9 July 1977 of Titans working on routes to East Park Drive. *Above:* Park Royal-bodied PD3A/1 No. 262 is seen outside the Haymarket Centre in Humberstone Gate West with No. 22 and a Metro-Scania behind. This section of road has since been pedestrianised. *Below:* Number 50 was a Metro-Cammell-bodied Leyland Titan which was new in 1966. It was photographed in Cort Crescent in the district of Braunstone to the west of the city and would have worked across the city centre to East Park Drive. A 1969 Austin Maxi completes the picture. Number 50 lasted in service until 1980.

Above: Number 202 was one of a batch of three Metro-Cammell-bodied Leyland PD3/1s which joined the fleet in 1960. It is seen in the garage yard on 21 September 1974. At the same time the department received five East Lancs-bodied PD3/1s; all eight buses were withdrawn in 1975. Alongside is MCW Scania No. 212, which was new in 1972 and lasted in service until 1986. LCT operated a fleet of thirty-four single-deck Scanias. *Below:* In 1965 LCT bought five AEC Renowns with East Lancs bodies with a further eight following the year after. No. 190 is seen in the depot yard on 3 March 1976; it was withdrawn later in the year. After serving with several independent operators it passed into preservation in 1992 and has since taken part in a number of rally events.

Above and below: Two more views recorded on 9 July 1977. *Above:* Metro-Cammell-bodied Leyland PD3A/1 No. 49 is seen waiting at the Melton Road terminus. The Melton Road route was originally operated by trams but only as far as Stafford Road; these were abandoned in favour of buses on 4 July 1949 and the route was subsequently extended. Industrial units have now been built on the adjacent land. *Below:* In the east of the city No. 84, a 1964 East Lancs-bodied Leyland PD3A/1, was pictured in Uppingham Road (A47) working towards the city centre. The garage on the left has since been replaced by a new residential development known as Chrisett Close. Just visible on the roof is a large fleet number. These were used to track the buses with a series of cameras over a wide expanse of the city centre with the images being relayed to the control centre at Rutland Street.

Above and below: 9 July 1977 is again the date when these two pictures were recorded. *Above*: Number 16 was one of the last Titans purchased by Leicester, in 1967, and was one of a batch of ten which carried East Lancs bodies. It is seen at the Nether Hall Road terminus of route 61. Little did anyone know at the time that in five years hence this bus would participate in the grand finale of the half-cabs at this very location. *Below*: Number 65 was a Park Royal-bodied Leyland PD3A/1 which was new in 1966. It is seen in Humberstone Gate East outside the Hansom Cab public house. This hostelry was previously known as The Champion, which was the name of the Derby winner in 1800, the year in which the pub was opened. Behind is the Old Black Lion (now Skandals Bar), which is even older and is believed to date from the 1770s.

Above and below: Two pictures recorded in East Park Road alongside Spinney Hills Park. Although these two buses are travelling in opposite directions to the same destination, they would work across the city centre and head for Braunstone. This section of road was once served by trams on a circular route but was converted to motorbus operation on 16 May 1949. *Above*: East Lancs-bodied Leyland PD3A/1 No. 17 working anti-clockwise on route 17. This bus worked until the final day of half-cabs in October 1982. *Below*: Metro-Cammell-bodied Titan No. 52, travelling in the opposite direction, has paused at the bus stop at the junction of Gwendolen Road. Number 52 was one of a large number of Titans, which were replaced by new Dennis Dominators in 1980/1.

Having worked across the city East Lancs-bodied Titan No. 23 is seen in leafy Hallam Crescent East at Braunstone on 9 July 1977. Longstanding route 18 still served this locality in 2022, by then operated by First Leicester, whose depot is situated in Abbey Lane, having replaced the former Leicester City Transport Abbey Park Road premises.

LCT bought just two AEC Renowns in 1965 which were bodied by East Lancs. One of the pair, No. 36, was photographed in the centre parking area at Humberstone Gate on 21 September 1974; it was withdrawn in 1976. This central area is no longer a bus park and has been paved over.

Above and below: Service 88 worked from Beaumont Leys in the north of the city to Eyres Monsell in the south via the city centre. Having commenced running to Eyres Monsell in January 1953 the southern section of the route still used the route number 88 in 2022. *Above*: Park Royal-bodied Leyland PD3A/1 No. 259 is seen waiting in Halifax Drive at Beaumont Leys on 9 July 1977; it was withdrawn later that year. *Below*: Later that day Metro-Cammell-bodied Titan No. 32 was photographed on the southern section of the route in Saffron Lane alongside Aylestone Recreational Ground. A new sports leisure centre was opened on the ground in 2020, thus changing the background of the view. The application of the LCT livery of cream and crimson was both simple and eye-catching, having changed from a reverse colour scheme back in the 1960s.

Seen in Horsefair Street waiting to leave for East Park Drive on 22 December 1978 is East Lancs-bodied Titan No. 73 with 1976 MCW Scania No. 166 behind. The adjacent buildings have since been demolished and replaced. On the side of the bus is an advert for Michael John Carpets, a business which was founded in 1946 and still going strong in 2022.

Park Royal-bodied No. 60 is seen in the Haymarket on 3 March 1976 also bound for East Park Drive. The adjacent building has been refurbished in the intervening years and is now a TK Max store. The advert on the side is for another carpet fitter which was perhaps a rival of Michael John in the 1970s. Number 60 is now preserved.

Above and below: The bus garage part of the Abbey Park Road complex was opened in 1926 and following further work in the 1930s it was capable of accommodating around 260 buses. *Above:* Four PD3A/1s were tucked away on 9 July 1977 with No. 265 being the odd one out in so much as it was bodied by Park Royal as opposed to East Lancashire Coachbuilders, who completed the other three, Nos 28, 74 and 71. *Below:* Titan Nos 25 and 63 were only a year apart in age and were bodied by East Lancs and Park Royal respectively. Standard number and destination displays have been fitted to both styles of bodywork. Alongside is ECW-bodied Bristol RE No. 128, which was one of a batch of twenty obtained in 1969. Note the hand trolley which may well have dated from the days of the trams. Sadly the depot closed after service on 12 May 2007 and was subsequently demolished.

East Lancs-bodied No. 93 is seen heading out of the city on the Melton Road service. Leonard Smith's Pharmacy of No. 195 Melton Road (on the extreme left) was still dispensing medicines in 2022. There is a date stone above the adjacent property that reads 1904, so the terrace row would have been seventy-three years old at the time.

Park Royal-bodied Titan No. 78 was also bound for Melton Road when photographed in the Haymarket on 9 July 1977. The Haymarket is now partly pedestrianised, although a bus stop still exists on the opposite side of the road. The ornate Memorial Clock dates back to 1868. Coincidentally there is also a memorial clock in the district of Haymarket in Edinburgh.

Above and below: *Above:* Seen on the Narborough Road at Braunstone on 9 July 1977, in the south of the city, is East Lancs-bodied Titan No. 71 on its journey north to the city centre and then beyond along the Melton Road to the city's northern extremity. *Below:* Christmas is coming, etc. 1966-built Park Royal-bodied Leyland PD3A/1 No. 56 was photographed in Humberstone Gate in 1978 just three days before the main event. Everything in the backdrop of this picture was demolished in the mid-1990s. The pedestrian footbridge used to connect the Haymarket Centre with Lewis's department store, which has been replaced with new retail outlets. Additionally the road has been pedestrianised.

Above and below: Present at the depot on 3 March 1976 were (above) 1964-built East Lancs-bodied Leyland PD3A/1 No. 89 and (below) Park Royal-bodied Leyland PD3/1 No. 401. This latter vehicle was in use as a Driver Tuition Vehicle at the time and had previously carried the fleet number 163. It was one of a batch of three obtained in 1958. Number 163 was another Leicester bus which made it into preservation. It was pensioned off by LCT in 1981 and after a stint in the north-west of England it was bought for preservation in 1995 and was initially restored in the mainly crimson livery. LCT changed from 'tin fronts' to 'St Helens' fronts from the 1961 deliveries.

Above and below: The final day of operation of Leicester's half-cabs was 2 October 1982 and
LCT didn't let the occasion pass without due ceremony. Leading up to the final day a number of
the 1967 vintage Leyland Titans gained side adverts proclaiming the forthcoming event. Their
replacements were to be ten East Lancs-bodied Dennis Dominators of which No. 67 behind was
one of them. Titan No. 28 is seen in Huberstone Gate on the last day. Occupying the adjacent
Victorian building is Greens Electricals; the building was originally attached to the Midlands
Distillery and was used by a wine merchant by the name of Challis & Allen. The building still
stands and has recently been refurbished. *Below*: Another Titan about to bow out was No. 33,
which is also seen in Humberstone Gate and is about to do a trip to Eyres Monsell. Note the
MCCW-bodied batch of PD3A/1s had illuminated side advert panels unlike the ones bodied by
East Lancs in the same year.

Leyland Titan No. 30 has run its last mile for Leicester City Transport and sits forlornly in the garage, still looking very smart.

Number 17 from the East Lancs-bodied batch waits in Humberstone Gate with new Dennis Dominator No. 65 behind. This Titan is now amongst the ranks of preserved Leicester City buses. Adjacent is the Secular Hall/ABC Ballroom, which opened on 5 March 1881 and is a Grade II listed building. Note the coin-slot Cadbury's chocolate bar dispensing machines on the wall. There is now an actual sweet shop in the adjacent part of the building.

LCT had a significantly sized parking lot in the city centre alongside the Rutland Street control centre. On the last day of half-cab operation Leyland Titan No. 32 was skulking in the yard alongside 1978 East Lancs-bodied Dennis Dominator No. 204. LCT vacated the site *c.* 1987 following bus deregulation but redevelopment work didn't take place until the mid-2000s.

The last day was somewhat miserable weather wise. Leyland Titan No. 31 stands at the Nether Hall terminus with its replacement, new Dennis Dominator No. 61, waiting to take over.

Above: Number 32 is seen again at the Nether Hall terminus. Another new Dominator can be seen waiting round the corner to take over. *Below:* The last rites fell to No. 16, which was suitably decked out for the run from the city centre to Nether Hall where it was replaced in service by Dominator No. 66. Note the addition of the third crimson band, which was applied specially for the occasion. Passengers/enthusiasts are seen transferring to the new bus for the run back to the city. This was not only Leicester's last half-cab but also the last of its type of any of the major operators in the Midlands. Number 16 was saved for preservation but was sadly destroyed in a barn fire, where it had been kept, in October 2011.

Northampton Corporation standardised their fleet on the Roe-bodied Daimler CVG6, buying small batches of the type virtually every year from 1957 to 1968. When this picture was recorded on 31 May 1977 No. 210 was the oldest of the type still in service, with Nos 200–9 having been replaced by Leyland Nationals in 1974. It is seen in Abington Street, approaching the junction of Mercers Row. Burton's Tailors is now the Skipton Building Society.

Most of the town's local services worked across the town centre, changing routes in the process. Number 259 of 1967 is seen in Eastfield Road on the Duston estate in the north-west of the town on 31 May 1977. The later vehicles had a wider/narrower destination screen. In 2022 this stop was served by Stagecoach local route 9.

Above and below: Two views recorded in Wellingborough Road on 31 May 1977. *Above:* No. 264 of 1968 is passing the junction of New Town Road. It is travelling towards the town centre from where it will then head off to Newton Road. Jean Cox Walk Round Store (yellow facia) is now occupied by Intersport. *Below:* Number 219 is being pursued by Daimler Roadliner No. 17. Note another variation in the livery application in that No. 219 has white lower deck window surrounds. Northampton Glassware Ltd on the corner of Adams Avenue is now occupied by Lighthouse Fish & Chips. The bunting is out for the Queen's Silver Jubilee celebrations, which at the time enveloped the country and would begin in earnest the following week.

Number 263 was one of the last batch of five CVG6s received in 1968. It is seen in Mare Fair on 31 May 1977. Across the road is A. Bell & Co., a home and lifestyle retailer that was established in 1898. They were still going strong in 2022 but had moved to Kingsthorpe Road whilst the above premises were now occupied by a mobile phone outlet.

Many of the local bus services started from on-street town centre bus stops. Number 248, with only a single white band, was photographed waiting in George Row on 29 April 1975 with a route 12 journey to Dallington Green. In 2022 this area of the town was served by Stagecoach local route 8 to King's Heath.

Seen on the same day, No. 261 was waiting in the Drapery. The adjacent bank has since turned into a coffee house. Since 1964 the Odeon had been playing host to the popular game of Bingo. The theatre opened way back in 1851 and was originally a Corn Exchange.

Number 246 was one of a batch of six buses received in 1965. In this view of the bus turning from Horse Market into Mare Fair on 31 May 1977 it looks as though it is not long out of the paintshop with white upper- and lower-deck window surrounds and 'Transport' fleetnames. Shock horror, the building behind is now painted pink and has modern-style windows.

Sporting a much older style of livery, No. 252 was photographed in Wood Hill, in the town centre, on 14 August 1976. It is setting out on route 6A to Newton Road. The House of Bewlay tobacconists in the background is now a Mace Convenience Store. The road network in the centre of Northampton has changed very little since these pictures were recorded.

Mercers Row played host to a number of bus stands. Daimler No. 257 is seen waiting to depart for Eastern Avenue on 29 April 1975. One of the department's twenty Daimler Roadliners, new in 1972/3, can be seen in the distance.

A broad nearside view of No. 220, which is seen in the Drapery on 31 May 1977. It is passing All Saints Plaza with Mercers Row trailing off in front of the bus. The *Chronicle & Echo* was the result of a merger between the *Northampton Daily Chronicle & Evening Herald* (est. 1880) and the *Daily Echo* (est. 1885) in 1931. Locally known as the 'Chron', it is now published once a week.

Number 247 of 1965 is seen in Ashbrow Road on the Briar Hill estate in the south-west of the town, again on 31 May 1977. The bus stop has been moved a short distance to accommodate a zebra crossing and new houses have been built to the front of the bus.

1966-built example No. 255 was photographed in Wood Hill on 29 April 1975. Demonstrating the continual change which takes place to town centre retail outlets, Burton's is now a jewellery shop and the adjacent building is occupied by Nandos.

Number 236 was photographed in the Drapery on 14 August 1976. The ranks of the CVG6s were decimated in 1977/8 with the acquisition of thirty-six Alexander-bodied Bristol VRTs, which other than the Leyland Nationals were Northampton's first major deviation from Daimler products. Rediffusion was a well-known television and radio rental company which as such ceased to exist in the late 1980s. The shop is now called 'Fever & Boutique'.

A busy scene in the Drapery on 29 April 1975 as four Daimlers can be seen on local town services. Behind No. 239 are Nos 236 and 244, whilst No. 212 is going away from the camera. The road layout here is much the same today, although restricted to buses and taxis. The two shops on the right (The Anglia and Ladbrokes) have been merged and are now known as The Auctioneer (a hostelry).

Also seen in the Drapery on 14 August 1976 is No. 217 of 1960. Another well-known high street shop brand can be seen on the right. Millets first opened a shop in Southampton in 1893. The chain started selling surplus army clothing after the First World War, in 1919, and continued to prosper. It was still going strong in 2022 but the branch had relocated to the Market Square.

1963-built model No. 239 is seen against a backdrop of late Victorian houses turning from Kingsley Road into St George's Avenue on 31 May 1977 on route 2 to Dallington Green via the town centre. Swift Electrical (front adverts) was still going strong from the same address in 2022.

On a quiet day in August 1976 1959-built example No. 211 is seen turning out of George Row into the Drapery. Another local business to avail themselves of advertising space was Jeffery, Sons & Co., who were founded in 1899 and at the time traded from No. 33 Gold Street in the town centre.

Number 241 is seen passing the White Elephant at the corner of St Matthew's Parade and Kingsley Road on 31 May 1977. The pub was opened in 1883 and was originally known as The Kingsley Park Hotel. Jeffrey's Furnishers have taken up more advert space on this Daimler. The town of Northampton is well known for shoe making and indeed the Football League club is known as the Cobblers. The town's population in 1981 was recorded as 157,217.

Number 219, new in 1960, is seen in East Park Parade alongside The Racecourse public park, heading away from the town centre. The date is again 31 May 1977. Many of these half-cab Daimlers would have been working their last months in service as the first of the new Bristol VRTs arrived in May with the balance of a large order towards the end of the year.

Above and below: The area known as The Headlands is a housing district situated in the north-east of the borough which was developed from the 1930s onwards through to the 1960s. The district was originally known as Cottarville. On 31 May 1977 these two pictures were captured of buses on route 15 in The Headlands thoroughfare. In the picture above No. 251 is passing house No. 185, which remains largely the same today, whilst below No. 238 is approaching the junction of Booth Lane South. Number 238 appears to have been spruced up from below the lower-deck windows. The area is now primarily served by Stagecoach local route 7.

Greyfriars bus station was opened in 1976 and was regarded by the townsfolk as a blot on the landscape. It closed in March 2014 and was demolished a year later. Number 258 is seen laying over on 31 March 1977. This bus is now semi-preserved and can often be seen at the Bowland Brewery in Clitheroe, Lancashire.

The last Daimler CVG6 received by Northampton was No. 267 in October 1968. A small number of the type survived the late 1970s cull and continued in service until January 1982. However, No. 267 was retained by the department for a further eleven years for special occasions. In 1993 it passed into preservation and has since attended many outdoor rally events. Timpson (Shoes) was founded in 1865 by William Timpson and is now part of a large company group. This particular shop is now Kaspa's.

Above and below: Nottingham City Transport (NCT) is a fairly large undertaking which in the past has operated trams, trolleybuses and buses. The large fleet has been variously garaged at six depots over the years of which Lower Parliament Street (LWP) and Trent Bridge were still functioning in 2022. By the early 1970s half-cab buses came in the shape of three different types – Park Royal-bodied AEC Regent Vs, AEC mainly Weymann-bodied Renowns and MCCW-bodied Leyland PD2/40s. The Renowns were the last of the configuration in service with the last of the type bowing out in 1976. *Above*: On 13 November 1975 East Lancs-bodied Renown No. 394 (former West Bridgeford UDC No. 42) was resting at the front of LWP garage. *Below*: PD2/40 No. 841 (renumbered from No. 41) was in use as a Driver Tuition Vehicle.

NCT operated a fleet of forty-four Renowns from 1965 to 1977. Number 368 was one of a large batch of thirty-five buses fitted with Weymann bodies. It was photographed in Middle Hill at the junction of Canal Street on 13 November 1975. To the right is the redundant formation of the Great Central Railway, which was closed in 1967 and is now the formation of the NET LRT line. Above the bus the spire of the High Pavement Chapel can be seen, which was founded in 1690. It is now a fine dining establishment.

Seven of the 1965 Renowns were fitted with bodies constructed by Northern Counties of Wigan. Number 392 is seen in Market Street in the city centre on 13 November 1975. The Nottingham Express Transit (NET) LRT line, which began operating in March 2004, now passes through this exact spot.

Another of the Weymann-bodied machines, No. 377, is seen in Milton Street on the same day. A long queue of passengers is waiting to board for the journey out to Carlton to the east of the city. This was around half a mile away from where Colwick (Netherfield) freight engine shed and extensive goods yards, which closed in their entirety in 1970, were located.

Between 1955 and 1957 NCT purchased sixty-five exposed-radiator Park Royal-bodied AEC Regent Vs, the last of which were withdrawn in 1976. Numbers 272/3 head two lines of Atlanteans in this view, which was recorded on Sunday 4 August 1974. As can be seen from the markings this area of LWP would normally function as a staff car park, which it still did in 2022.

A timeless scene in Lower Parliament Street as in the intervening forty-seven years only the buses have changed. They are Weymann-bodied Renown No. 382 and 1966 Met-Cam Daimler CRG No. 113, modelled on the distinctive Nottingham design of the period (bodies built by different manufacturers were made to look similar for ease of maintenance). Note the Fleetline was one year older than the AEC.

The final example photographed on 13 November 1975 was No. 361, which is seen in Long Row West. The Nottingham fleet was always well turned out and even a twelve-year-old bus could be made to look smart. Route 75 worked from Bulwell (Crabtree Estate) in the north of the city, through the city centre to Trent Bridge.

NBC Midland Red had a strong presence in Leicester and worked out of a garage in Sandiacre Street. BMMO D9 No. 5423 of 1966 vintage was photographed at the New Parks terminus, off the Glenfield Road roundabout, on 9 July 1977. Number 5423 was withdrawn the following year whilst the garage closed in 1996.

BMMO D9s Nos 5345 and 5418 are seen in Charles Street in the centre of Leicester on the same day, with the latter heading for New Parks. Number 5345 was withdrawn later that month with No. 5418 lasting until the end of the year. The footbridge in the background was closed in 1997 and removed in 2007. The adjacent buildings have been demolished and were replaced by a bus station, which opened in 1994. This was later completely rebuilt and reopened in 2016.

BMMO D9 No. 5362 was new in 1963 and is seen running empty in Humberstone Gate East in the centre of Leicester. Behind the bus is the Hansom Cab public house.

St Margaret's bus station with its distinctive concrete bus shelters was a prominent feature in Leicester for many years. The use of the site dates from the 1940s, although what can be seen above was swept away in the mid-1980s when the station was rebuilt to a more modern design. That in turn was also replaced when it was further modernised in 2007 and then replaced again by a state-of-the-art complex, which opened in June 2022. BMMO D9 No. 5311 is waiting to leave on a service for Hungarton, which is around 7 miles to the east of the city. Leyland National No. 156 is keeping the D9 company.

W. Gash & Sons Ltd of Newark was a long established operator whose buses could be seen on a regular basis in Nottingham. KAL 578 was a Daimler CVD6 which was originally new in 1948 with a Strachan body. It was fitted with a new Massey body in 1962. It was photographed on the outskirts of Nottingham on 10 November 1979. Gash was acquired by the Yorkshire Traction Group in 1989 and the Daimler passed with the operator to the Lincolnshire Road Car Company. It is now preserved.

Another independent operator close to Nottingham was the South Notts Bus Company, founded in 1926 and based in the village of Gotham. South Notts was bought out by Nottingham CT in March 1991 and the garage remained in use until 27 March 2021. On 20 November 1983 low-height Northern Counties-bodied Leyland PD3/4 80 NVO, which had been purchased new in 1962, was one of a number of half-cabs to be found in the yard.

Stevensons of Uttoxeter was founded in 1926 and established a depot in the nearby small hamlet of Spath. They were renowned for the variety of second-hand buses operated. RCN 699 was a Park Royal-bodied AEC Routemaster which was originally new to Northern General in 1964. It is seen in the garage yard on 20 November 1983. This site and former garage buildings are now occupied by Spath Garage Motor Services.

DFC 365D had been acquired from City of Oxford and was a Park Royal-bodied AEC Renown. On 24 May 1975 it was to be found in Burton's Wetmore Road bus station (no trace of which now remains) on a service to Uttoxeter. Stevensons merged with East Staffordshire District Council on 1 October 1985.

Bibliography

Malcolm Keeley, *West Midlands* (Harrow Weald, Capital Transport, 1988).

M. Keeley, M. Russell & P. Gray, *Birmingham City Transport* (Glossop, Transport Publishing Company, 1977).

F. P. Groves, *Nottingham City Transport* (Glossop, Transport Publishing Company, 1978).

Peter Gould online Local Transport Histories.